Colors

Orange

Nancy Harris

Heinemann Library
Chicago, Illinois

HEINEMANN-RAINTREE

TO ORDER:
☎ Call Customer Service (Toll-Free) **1-888-454-2279**
🖥 Visit **heinemannraintree.com** to browse our catalog and order online.

Editorial: Rebecca Rissman
Design: Kimberly R. Miracle and Joanna Hinton-Malivoire
Photo Research: Tracy Cummins and Tracey Engel
Production: Duncan Gilbert

Originated by Dot
Printed and bound by South China Printing Company
The paper used to print this book comes from sustainable resources.

ISBN-13: 978-1-4329-1588-9 (hc)
ISBN-10: 1-4329-1588-6 (hc)
ISBN-13: 978-1-4329-1598-8 (pb)
ISBN-10: 1-4329-1598-3 (pb)

12 11 10 09 08
10 9 8 7 6 5 4 3 2 1

Library of Congress
Cataloging-in-Publication Data
Harris, Nancy, 1956-
  Orange / Nancy Harris.
    p. cm. -- (Colors)   7728
Includes bibliographical references and index.
  ISBN 978-1-4329-1588-9 (hc) -- ISBN 978-1-4329-1598-8 (pb)
  1. Orange (Color)--Juvenile literature. 2. Color--Juvenile literature.
  I. Title. QC495.5.H376 2008
  535.6--dc22
                        2008005606

Acknowledgments
The author and publisher are grateful to the following for permission to reproduce copyright material: ©Alamy **p. 8** (Donna Strathy); ©CORBIS **pp. 5** Bottom Right, **20, 22d, 23b** (Chase Jarvis), **14, 23a** (Hal Beral); ©Index Stock Imagery **p. 9** (DesignPics Inc.); ©istockphoto **pp. 5** Bottom Center (Steve Dibblee), **5** Top Right (Viktor Neimanis), **13** (Michael Sacco), **16** (Dirk Freder); ©Photos.com p. **21**; ©Shutterstock **pp. 4** Bottom Center (silvano audisio), **4** Bottom Left (Maceofoto), **4** Bottom Right (John Bell), **4** Top Center (misha shiyanov), **4** Top Left, **10, 22a** (Otmar Smit), **4 Top Right** (beltsazar), **5** Bottom Left (aaaah), **5** Top Center (Filip Fuxa), **5** Top Left, **18, 22c** (Steve Cukrov), **6** (Maxim Tupikov), **7** (Péter Gudella), **11** (slowfish), **15** (kristian sekulic), **17** (Keith Levit), **19** (Jose Fuente); ©SuperStock **pp. 12, 22b** (age fotostock).

Cover photograph reproduced with permission of ©Getty Images/Minden Pictures/Michael & Patricia Fogden.

Back cover photograph reproduced with permission of ©Shutterstock/Steve Cukrov.

The publishers would like to thank Nancy Harris for her assistance in the preparation of this book.

Every effort has been made to contact copyright holders of any material reproduced in this book. Any omissions will be rectified in subsequent printings if notice is given to the publisher.

Disclaimer
All the Internet addresses (URLs) given in this book were valid at the time of going to press. However, due to the dynamic nature of the Internet, some addresses may have changed, or sites may have changed or ceased to exist since publication. While the author and publisher regret any inconvenience this may cause readers, no responsibility for any such changes can be accepted by either the author or the publisher.

Contents

Orange

Are all plants orange?

Are all animals orange?

Are all rocks orange?

Are all soils orange?

Plants

Some leaves are orange.

Some leaves are not orange.

he stems are orange.

Some stems are not orange.

Some flowers are orange.

Some flowers are not orange.

Animals

Some feathers are orange.

Some feathers are not orange.

Some scales are orange.

Some scales are not orange.

Some fur is orange.

Some fur is not orange.

Rocks

Some rocks are orange.

Some rocks are not orange.

Soil

Some soil is orange.

Some soil is not orange.

What Have You Learned?

Some plants are orange.

Some animals are orange.

Some rocks are orange.

Some soil is orange.

Picture Glossary

scale small plate that covers the body of some animals

soil mix of small rocks and dead plants. Plants grow in soil.

Index

Note to Parents and Teachers

Before reading:
Talk with children about colors. Explain that there are many different colors, and that each color has a name. Use a color wheel or other simple color chart to point to name each color. Then, ask children to make a list of the colors they can see. After they have completed their list, ask children to share their results.

After reading:
Ask students to make a poster for the color orange. Help them to write the word orange at the top of a piece of paper, then encourage them to brainstorm for orange objects that they can draw on their poster. Then, ask each student to share their posters with the rest of the class.